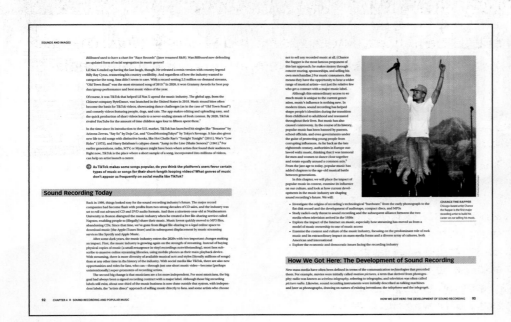

Centered in the "now," with just the right balance between today and yesterday. Each chapter begins with a new section on the latest developments in the industry (a look at where we are now) before examining key topics in the industry's history and why they're important (a look at how we got here). Chapters connect historical developments to current technologies and cultural touchstones whenever possible to further illustrate the relationship between past and present.

An engaging digital learning experience with LaunchPad. LaunchPad for *Media & Culture* merges and converges print and digital to enhance your learning experience in an all-in-one learning platform with the e-book, assessment, study and critical thinking tools, and more.

- Gamelike **LearningCurve quizzes** reinforce learning of chapter material and **digital flash cards** help you review key terms and concepts.
- A digital version of the new case study **A Guide to Identifying Fake News,** which examines misinformation in our current media environment, includes a survey activity you can use to assess the credibility of a story.
- A rich library of **videos** offers easy access to clips from movies, TV shows, interviews, and more.
- **Media Literacy Activities** encourage you to apply and practice your media literacy skills.
- LaunchPad's **career unit** features video activities, relevant resources, and a new edition of the *Media Career Guide: Preparing for Jobs in the 21st Century* e-book, which is packed with practical information for students considering a major in the media industries.

MEDIA CAREER GUIDE
Preparing for Jobs in the 21st Century
Thirteenth Edition

Sherri Hope Culver
Nichole Harken

LaunchPad
macmillan learning
launchpadworks.com

Black Panther on Film
The citizens of Wakanda decide whether to challenge Prince T'Challa for the throne in this clip from the Ryan Coogler film.

Discussion: What does this clip tell us about formal elements of the film *Black Panther*, including its narrative (story structure, characters, themes), genre, and production design?

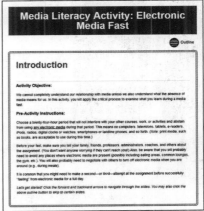

Media Literacy Activity: Electronic Media Fast

Outline

Introduction

Activity Objective:

We cannot completely understand our relationship with media unless we also understand what the absence of media means for us. In this activity, you will apply the critical process to examine what you learn during a media fast.

Pre-Activity Instructions:

Choose a twenty-four-hour period that will not interfere with your other courses, work, or activities and abstain from using *any electronic media* during that period. This means no computers, televisions, tablets, e-readers, iPods, radios, digital clocks or watches, smartphones or landline phones, and so forth. (Note: print media, such as books, are acceptable to use during this time.)

Before your fast, make sure you tell your family, friends, professors, administrators, coaches, and others about the assignment. (You don't want anyone worrying if they can't reach you!) Also, be aware that you will probably need to avoid any places where electronic media are present (possibly including eating areas, common lounges, the gym, etc.). You will also probably need to negotiate with others to turn off electronic media when you are around (e.g., during meals).

It is common that you might need to make a second—or third—attempt at the assignment before successfully 'fasting' from electronic media for a full day.

Let's get started! Click the forward and backward arrows to navigate through the slides. You may also click the above outline button to skip to certain slides.

Media & Culture's critical and cultural perspective and engaging media stories tie all of this material together, addressing the importance of history, the digital revolution, and media literacy.

PRAISE FOR MEDIA & CULTURE

It is simply the best intro to mass communication book available.

Matthew Cecil, *Wichita State University*

For myself and my students, the simple truth is that this is the best textbook we have ever used in my twenty years of teaching. This textbook covers the issues of media and culture in both scholarly and down-to-earth ways.

Hsin-I Liu, *University of the Incarnate Word*

It's a well-written, up-to-date book. It successfully walks the line between providing in-depth information and engaging students with fresh examples.

Richard Craig, *San José State University*

I love the media literacy activities. We do as many as we can in class. It is helpful for the students to see how to work through a topic from a critical perspective.

Andrea Mason, *Arapahoe Community College*

I love *Media & Culture*! I have used it since the first edition. *Media & Culture* integrates the history of a particular medium or media concept with the culture, economics, and technological advances of the time. But more than that, the authors are explicit in their philosophy that media and culture cannot be separated.

Deborah Larson, *Missouri State University*

Media & Culture respects students' opinions while challenging them to take more responsibility and to be accountable for their media choices. This text is essential for professors who are truly committed to teaching students how to understand the media.

Drew Jacobs, *Camden County College*

I have always been impressed with how up-to-date this textbook has been. The discussions of TikTok and COVID-19 are really helpful in ensuring that students recognize they are not reading your average stale textbook.

David Wolfgang, *Colorado State University–Fort Collins*

It's an outstanding text, and the media literacy thread that runs through it absolutely can't be beat.

Jodi Hallsten Lyczak, *Illinois State University*

MEDIA & CULTURE
Mass Communication in a Digital Age

Thirteenth Edition

Richard Campbell

Miami University

Christopher R. Martin

University of Northern Iowa

Bettina Fabos

University of Northern Iowa

Ron Becker

Miami University

bedford/st.martin's
Macmillan Learning
Boston | New York

"WE ARE NOT ALONE."
For my family—Reese, Chris, Caitlin, and Dianna

"YOU MAY SAY I'M A DREAMER, BUT I'M NOT THE ONLY ONE."
For our daughters—Olivia and Sabine

"ALONE WE CAN DO LITTLE, TOGETHER WE CAN DO MUCH."
For my husband—Marc

For Bedford/St. Martin's

Vice President, Editorial, Macmillan Learning Humanities: Leasa Burton
Senior Program Director for Communication and College Success: Erika Gutierrez
Director of Content Development: Jane Knetzger
Senior Developmental Editor: Christina Lembo
Associate Editor: Kathy McInerney
Director of Media Editorial: Adam Whitehurst
Media Editor: Nicole Erazo
Executive Marketing Manager: Scott Guile
Marketing Assistant: Mara Natale
Senior Director, Content Management Enhancement: Tracey Kuehn
Senior Managing Editor: Lisa Kinne
Senior Content Project Manager: Edward Dionne
Senior Workflow Project Manager: Jennifer Wetzel
Production Supervisor: Brianna Lester
Director of Design, Content Management: Diana Blume
Interior Design: Maureen McCutcheon
Cover Design: William Boardman
Art Manager: Matthew McAdams
Director of Rights and Permissions: Hilary Newman
Photo Researcher: Krystyna Borgen, Lumina Datamatics, Inc.
Permissions Editor: Allison Ziebka-Viering
Director of Digital Production: Keri deManigold
Advanced Media Project Manager: Sarah O'Connor Kepes
Copy Editor: Jamie Thaman
Composition: Lumina Datamatics, Inc.
Cover Image: Kevin Kozicki/Image Source/Getty Images
Printing and Binding: LSC Willard

Library of Congress Control Number: 2021941299

ISBN 978-1-319-24493-4 (Paperback)
ISBN 978-1-319-36571-4 (Loose-leaf Edition)

Printed in the United States of America.

2   3   4   5   26   25   24   23   22

Acknowledgments
Acknowledgments and copyrights appear on the same page as the text and art selections they cover; these acknowledgments and copyrights constitute an extension of the copyright page.

At the time of publication, all Internet URLs published in this text were found to accurately link to their intended website.

For information, write: Bedford/St. Martin's, 75 Arlington Street, Boston, MA 02116

About the Authors

RICHARD CAMPBELL is professor emeritus and founding chair of the Department of Media, Journalism, and Film at Miami University, as well as the 2019 recipient of the university's Benjamin Harrison Medallion for Outstanding Contribution to the Education of the Nation. Campbell is the author of *"60 Minutes" and the News: A Mythology for Middle America* (1991) and coauthor of *Cracked Coverage: Television News, the Anti-Cocaine Crusade, and the Reagan Legacy* (1994). He has written for numerous publications, including *Columbia Journalism Review, Critical Studies in Mass Communication,* and *TV Quarterly.* Campbell is cocreator of *Stats+Stories,* a long-running podcast sponsored by Miami University and the American Statistical Association, and winner of the 2021 Communication Award from the Mathematical Association of America. His other projects include the digital *Oxford Observer* newspaper and Report for Ohio, initiatives aimed at getting more young journalists real-world experience covering underreported areas in rural and urban communities. He is executive producer of a 2019 documentary on the role that Oxford, Ohio, played in 1964's Freedom Summer, titled *Training for Freedom: How Ordinary People in an Unusual Time and Unlikely Place Made Extraordinary History.* He served for ten years on the board of directors for Cincinnati Public Radio and holds a PhD from Northwestern University.

Photo credit: Dianna Campbell

CHRISTOPHER R. MARTIN is a professor of digital journalism and former department head of the Department of Communication and Media at the University of Northern Iowa. He is author of two award-winning books on labor and the media: *No Longer Newsworthy: How the Mainstream Media Abandoned the Working Class* and *Framed! Labor and the Corporate Media,* both with Cornell University Press. He has written articles, book chapters, and reviews on journalism, televised sports, the Internet, and labor for several publications, including *Communication Research; Journal of Communication; Journal of Communication Inquiry; Labor Studies Journal; Culture, Sport, and Society; NiemanReports;* and *Perspectives on Politics.* He is also on the editorial board of the *Journal of Communication Inquiry.* He is a contributing scholar to the Center for Journalism and Liberty and a regular contributor to *Working-Class Perspectives.* Martin holds a PhD from the University of Michigan and has also taught at Miami University.

Photo credit: Bettina Fabos

BETTINA FABOS is a professor of visual communication and interactive digital studies at the University of Northern Iowa. She is the executive producer of the interactive web photo history *Proud and Torn: A Visual Memoir of Hungarian History* (proudandtorn.org); the cofounder of a public digital archive of Iowa family snapshots, Fortepan Iowa (fortepan.us); and a champion of the Creative Commons. Fabos has also written extensively about critical media literacy, Internet commercialization, the role of the Internet in education, and media representations of popular culture. Her work has been published in *Visual Communication Quarterly, Library Trends, Review of Educational Research,* and *Harvard Educational Review,* and she has received numerous awards for her creative work. Fabos has also taught at Miami University and has a PhD from the University of Iowa.

Photo credit: Christopher Martin

RON BECKER is a professor of media and communication and strategic communication at Miami University. He is the author of *Gay TV and Straight America* (Rutgers University Press) and coeditor of *Saturday Night Live and American TV* (Indiana University Press). His work has also appeared in publications like *The Craft of Criticism; The Television Studies Reader; How to Watch TV; Reading the Bromance; The Velvet Light Trap; Queer Studies in Media and Popular Culture;* and *Historical Journal of Film, Radio and Television.* Becker holds a PhD from the University of Wisconsin–Madison.

Photo credit: Marc Loy

Brief Contents

1 Media, Culture, and Communication: A Critical Approach *3*

PART 1: INTERACTIVE MEDIA

2 The Internet and Digital Media *33*

3 Digital Gaming and the Media Playground *59*

PART 2: SOUNDS AND IMAGES

4 Sound Recording and Popular Music *91*

5 Popular Radio and the Origins of Broadcasting *123*

6 Television: From Broadcasting to Streaming *157*

7 Movies and the Power of Images *193*

PART 3: WORDS AND PICTURES

8 Newspapers: The Rise and Decline of Modern Journalism *225*

9 Magazines in the Age of Specialization *257*

10 Books and the Power of Print *283*

PART 4: THE BUSINESS OF MASS MEDIA

11 Advertising and Commercial Culture *309*

12 Public Relations and Framing the Message *343*

13 Media Economics and the Global Marketplace *367*

PART 5: DEMOCRATIC EXPRESSION AND THE MASS MEDIA

14 The Culture of Journalism: Values, Ethics, and Democracy *399*

15 Media Effects and Cultural Approaches to Research *429*

16 Legal Controls and Freedom of Expression *455*

CASE STUDY: A Guide to Identifying Fake News *485*

Preface

This is an exciting and tumultuous time in the media. Developing an understanding of mass communication and becoming a critical consumer and producer of the media is vitally important—especially now, as many media institutions are being upended, as our engagement with media seems to sort us into increasingly isolated niches, and as the lines between fact and fiction are being continuously blurred. *Media & Culture* reaches students where they are and puts the media industries into perspective both historically and culturally, helping students become more informed citizens who use critical thinking and media literacy skills in a variety of ways and via a variety of media, even as they are being bombarded by information.

While today's students have integrated digital media into their daily lives (and may even be addicted to their mobile phones), they may not understand how the media evolved to this point; how technology converges text, audio, and visual media; and what all these developments mean. This is why we believe that the critical and cultural perspectives at the core of *Media & Culture*'s approach are more important than ever. *Media & Culture* pulls back the curtain to show students how the media really work—from the roots and economics of each media industry to the implications of today's consolidated media ownership to how these industries have changed in our digital world. By looking at the full history of media through a critical lens, students will leave this course with a better understanding of the complex relationship between the media and our continually evolving culture.

These core principles remain in place in this thirteenth edition, accompanied by a number of new developments. First and foremost, it is with this edition that we wish a happy retirement to founding author Richard Campbell, who with *Media & Culture* reinvented what a mass media textbook could be. His beautiful narrative storytelling is the soul of *Media & Culture* and helped make it a textbook that students love to read. We also welcome Ron Becker to the project, who brings energy, enthusiasm, and his complementary research background. Together we are a team of authors with a deep love and understanding of our media landscape. Every semester we teach this book's material in our respective classrooms, often learning about the latest trends from our many students. We also contribute our own specialties to *Media & Culture*: Chris is an expert on journalism and media coverage of labor unions and the working class, Bettina combines her strong background in visual communication (video production and web development) with an expertise in online public archiving, and Ron's scholarship is tied to television-film studies, cultural theory, and LGBTQ+ representation.

Together we have focused on making a number of exciting updates to this thirteenth edition, including a reframing to reflect the reality of our digital world. In exploring the impact of the digital revolution in more depth than ever before, the new edition digs into the reality of what it means to live, work, and communicate in today's connected world, where digital is the norm and media industries must be digital in order to survive. By moving away from the idea that convergence is something new and different, the thirteenth edition focuses more intently on the role of digital media in everyday life, including how the digital world affects us as individuals and as a society. In Chapter 1, for example, we explore the development of *masspersonal* communication, where elements of both interpersonal and mass communication converge through our use of mobile phones and social media; we look at the power and ubiquity of the media environment that surrounds us every day; and we consider the viewing practices, participation, and fragmentation that characterize our current media culture. In Chapter 2, we examine the complexities that emerge from three key features of digital technology: the decentralization of information, the growth of online communities, and the ease with which we can manipulate digital content. In Chapters 3, 4, 5, 6, and 7, we look at the rapid growth of streaming and the myriad ways its dominance has influenced digital games, music, radio, TV, and movies. And in Chapter 11, we consider how the latest in digital marketing techniques, including single sign-on and predictive marketing, are affecting our personal data profiles.

In developing the thirteenth edition of *Media & Culture*, we have focused on achieving just the right balance of concepts from today and yesterday. While an examination of media history continues to be a core feature of the text, as it has been since the first edition, coverage of current topics that relate directly to students' lives, interests, and experiences in today's digital world receives equal emphasis. Each chapter begins with a new section on the latest developments in the industry today (a look at where we are now) before examining key topics in the industry's history and why they're important (a look at how we got here). Chapter 1 also includes a new subsection explaining why historical information is included in the text, and chapters connect historical developments to current technologies and modern cultural touchstones whenever possible to better illustrate the relationship between past and present.

Media & Culture shares stories about the history of media, the digital revolution, and technological convergence—and the book itself practices convergence, too. The thirteenth edition is available in LaunchPad, Macmillan's digital platform, which includes an interactive e-book featuring dozens of video activities that complement text coverage (including clips from movies like *Black Panther* and *Star Wars: The Last Jedi* and television shows like *13 Reasons Why*), our acclaimed LearningCurve adaptive quizzing, new digital flash cards, interactive Media Literacy Activities, and a career unit for students interested in a future in media—along with quizzes, activities, and instructor resources.

Of course, *Media & Culture* retains its well-loved and teachable organization, which supports instructors in their quest to provide students with a clear understanding of the historical and cultural contexts for each media industry. Our signature five-step critical process for studying the media has struck a chord with hundreds of instructors and thousands of students across the United States and North America. We continue to be enthusiastic about—and humbled by—the chance to work with the amazing community of teachers that has developed around *Media & Culture*. We hope the text enables students to become more knowledgeable media consumers and engaged, media-literate citizens who are ready to take a critical role in shaping our dynamic world.

The Thirteenth Edition of *Media & Culture* Navigates Today's Hyperfast Media Landscape

Media & Culture has experienced the digital revolution, and the thirteenth edition continues to keep pace with the technological, economic, and social effects of today's rapidly changing media landscape. Since the publication of the twelfth edition, we've seen more changes than ever: the significant and lasting impact of the coronavirus pandemic on media use and development; media coverage of national and global protests for racial justice; the 2020 presidential election and its aftermath; ongoing issues of social media privacy, fraud, and disinformation; and so on. The thirteenth edition of *Media & Culture* covers all this and more.

A Reframing to Reflect the Reality of Our Digital World

Rather than approaching the digital revolution as an ongoing realignment that we are just beginning to understand, *Media & Culture*, Thirteenth Edition, acknowledges that digital media culture is firmly established in today's world and takes steps to analyze and explore what this means and why it matters. This edition focuses more intently on the presence and meaning of digital media in everyday life, including how the digital world affects us all as individuals and as a larger society.

- **Chapter 1** has been thoroughly revised and includes new discussion about the development of *masspersonal* communication, where elements of both interpersonal and mass communication converge through our use of mobile phones and social media; the power and ubiquity of the media environment that surrounds us; and the viewing practices, participation, and fragmentation that characterize media culture in our digital era.
- **Chapter 2** has been reconceptualized to spotlight the complex dynamics of media and communication in the digital era, including the complexities that emerge from three key features of digital technology: its decentralization of the creation and sharing of information, how it helps

us build online communities, and how it enables us to manipulate information. In addition, a new section looks at the numerous factors linked to companies' and governments' efforts to control data and Internet access.

- **Additional areas of relevant discussion** include a look at the rapid growth of streaming and the myriad ways its dominance has affected digital games, music, radio, TV, and movies today (Chapters 3, 4, 5, 6, and 7); an exploration of what it takes for newspapers to succeed in the digital era, including the new platforms that are being invented to do the work of newspaper journalism (Chapter 8); the latest in digital marketing, including single sign-on, predictive marketing, advertising via wearables and Internet of Things devices, and an increasing emphasis on influencers (Chapter 11); and the corporate takeovers and mergers that characterize today's media conglomerates in their pursuit of vertical integration, horizontal integration, and synergy (Chapter 13).

Centered in the Now, with a Better Balance between Today and Yesterday

From its first edition, *Media & Culture*'s approach has been to hook students in with the media they know most, like the Internet and digital gaming, before diving into older forms of media, like books and newspapers. While an examination of media history continues to be a core feature of the text, we believe that engaging students in the now will strengthen their interest in understanding the perspective provided by historical material and its relationship to the present moment. The thirteenth edition achieves the ideal balance of coverage between yesterday and today with these features:

- **Spotlighting today's most intriguing media topics.** The thirteenth edition includes more coverage of topics that relate directly to students' lives, interests, and experiences in today's digital world. Each chapter begins with a new section on the latest developments in the industry today (a look at where we are now) before examining key topics in the industry's history and why they're important (a look at how we got here). Associated iClicker questions about the chapter-opening discussion engage students in the material from the outset to get them excited about what's to come.

- **Explaining history's importance.** Chapter 1 includes a new subsection about why historical information is included in the text, with a direct explanation of how understanding history prompts critical thinking and provides insight into today's media world.

- **Focusing on relevance and making connections to currency.** The historical coverage has been refocused to highlight only the most important and relevant content in each chapter, which keeps the discussion clear and meaningful. In addition, chapters connect historical developments to current technologies and modern cultural touchstones whenever possible to further illustrate the relationship between the past and the present.

Increased Emphasis on Representation and Diverse Voices

This thirteenth edition further extends a key theme that has long been emphasized in *Media & Culture*: the importance of representation and the value of including diverse viewpoints, images, and experiences in our exploration of the media. New and expanded coverage includes a section on the politics of representation and the impact of media portrayals (Chapter 1); an examination of the racial biases woven into algorithms that increasingly guide the way we live (Chapter 2); an expanded discussion of gender and racial diversity in digital gaming (Chapter 3); a new section on the importance of gay material and the quality audience during television's post-network era (Chapter 6); a discussion of how journalistic objectivity and newsroom diversity are being reconsidered in light of the racial justice movement (Chapters 8 and 14); new historical images spotlighting the work of a variety of individuals who played foundational roles in media's development, including voice actor Jack Gibson and filmmaker Oscar Micheaux (Chapters 5 and 7); and much more.

New and Expanded Frameworks for Media Analysis

Accessible models in Chapter 1 prompt students to reflect on the meaning, impact, and importance of media use—in their own lives and in our society as a whole. New to the thirteenth edition, the three-roles framework helps students think critically about their roles as media producers, media consumers, and media citizens, including how these roles intersect and compete. In addition, an expanded discussion of the cultural model, one of the hallmarks of the book, explores the interconnections between media texts, industries, technologies, users, and the cultural context within which they are embedded.

Coverage of Key Media Developments

Each chapter explores and analyzes the latest media issues, prompting students to reflect on how recent developments affect media and our society. These include the exponential growth of at-home businesses like streaming and digital gaming during the COVID-19 pandemic, as well as the resulting financial struggles of newspapers without advertisers and theaters without moviegoers; media coverage of the protests for racial justice around both the country and the world; the use and abuse of social media platforms and the proliferation of fake news (including a survey activity that students can use to assess the credibility of news stories for themselves); the 2020 presidential election and its aftermath; consumer privacy and targeted online advertising; the rise of conservative media; and an "overdue reckoning" on the norms of journalistic objectivity in the mainstream media.

Print and Media Converge with LaunchPad in Brand-New Ways

LaunchPad for *Media & Culture* merges and converges the book with the web.

- **LearningCurve adaptive quizzing** helps students review important concepts from each chapter. LearningCurve includes multiple-choice questions at different levels of difficulty, hints, feedback, and links to e-book material for easy reference.

- **A variety of video activities** that complement text coverage—including clips from movies like *Black Panther* and *Star Wars: The Last Jedi* and television shows like *13 Reasons Why*—gets students thinking critically about media texts.

- **A digital version of the text's new case study on fake news** examines the history, definition, and typology of misinformation in our current media environment. Carefully crafted to spotlight useful source standards without getting into partisan arguments, the guide incorporates the critical process and includes a survey activity that students can use to assess the credibility of a story for themselves.

- **A career unit**, which includes the newly updated *Media Career Guide: Preparing for Jobs in the 21st Century*, helps students on the path toward exploring and realizing their future career goals.

- In addition, LaunchPad offers a wealth of **engagement and study tools**—including iClicker questions that hook students into each chapter, new digital flash cards that students can use to review key terms and concepts, chapter quizzes, media literacy activities, and other assessments, along with the e-book—and, for instructors, a complete set of supplements to support teaching, whether that is in person, online, or via a hybrid approach.

For more ideas on how using LaunchPad can enhance your course, see the Instructor's Resource Manual. For a list of available video clips and access information, see the last book page and the inside back cover or visit **launchpadworks.com**.

Hallmark Features: *Media & Culture* Provides a Critical, Cultural, Comprehensive, and Compelling Introduction to the Mass Media

- **A critical approach to media literacy.** *Media & Culture* introduces students to five stages of the critical-thinking and writing process—description, analysis, interpretation, evaluation, and engagement. The text uses these stages as a lens for examining the historical context and current processes that shape mass media as part of our culture. This framework informs the writing throughout, including the Media Literacy and the Critical Process feature in every chapter.

Online interactive Media Literacy Activities give students even more practice in developing their media literacy and critical-thinking skills.

- **A cultural perspective.** The text focuses on the vital relationship between the mass media and our shared culture—how cultural trends influence the mass media, and how specific historical developments, technical innovations, and key decision makers in the history of the media have affected the ways our democracy and society have evolved.

- **Comprehensive coverage.** The text supports the instructor in providing students with the nuts-and-bolts content they need to understand each media industry's history, organizational structure, economic models, and market statistics.

- **An exploration of media economics and democracy.** *Media & Culture* spotlights the significance and impact of multinational media systems throughout the text. It also invites students to explore the implications of the Telecommunications Act of 1996, net neutrality, Section 230 of the Communications Decency Act, and other media regulations. Additionally, each chapter ends with a discussion of the effects of particular mass media on the nature of democratic life.

- **Compelling storytelling.** Most mass media make use of storytelling to tap into our shared beliefs and values, and so does *Media & Culture*. Each chapter presents the events and issues surrounding media culture as intriguing and informative narratives rather than a series of unconnected facts and feats, mapping the accompanying—and often uneasy—changes in consumer culture and democratic society.

- **The most accessible book available.** Learning tools in every chapter help students find and remember the information they need to know. Bulleted lists at the beginning of every chapter give students a road map to key concepts, Media Literacy and the Critical Process boxes model the five-step critical process, Examining Ethics and Global Village boxes spotlight key ethical and global issues, and Chapter Reviews help students study for quizzes and exams and set them up for success.

Digital Options

Whether it's LaunchPad, an e-book, or a printed version, choose the best format for you. For more information on these resources, please visit the online catalog at **macmillanlearning.com**, or visit the Macmillan Learning Student Store at **store.macmillanlearning.com**.

- **LaunchPad for *Media & Culture*, Thirteenth Edition.** LaunchPad is a digital platform that dramatically enhances teaching and learning—and that can be integrated with campus learning management systems. LaunchPad combines the full e-book with video activities, LearningCurve adaptive quizzing, a career unit, Media Literacy Activities, a test bank, chapter quizzes, and instructor's resources. To order LaunchPad for *Media & Culture* on its own, use **ISBN 978-1-319-36575-2**. To order LaunchPad packaged with the loose-leaf version of *Media & Culture*, use **ISBN 978-1-319-47750-9**. To order LaunchPad packaged with the print version of *Media & Culture*, use **ISBN 978-1-319-47748-6**.

- **E-books.** *Media & Culture* is available in a range of e-book formats for use on computers, tablets, and e-readers. See **macmillanlearning.com** to learn more.

Student Resources

For more information on student resources or to learn about package options, please visit the online catalog at **macmillanlearning.com**.

LaunchPad for *Media & Culture*: Where Students Learn

Digital tools for *Media & Culture*, Thirteenth Edition, are available on LaunchPad, a dynamic online platform that combines a curated collection of videos, homework assignments, e-book content, and the LearningCurve adaptive quizzing program, organized for easy assignability, in a simple user interface. LaunchPad for *Media & Culture* features:

- **A fully interactive e-book.** Every LaunchPad e-book comes with powerful study tools, multimedia content, and easy customization options for instructors. Students can search, highlight, and bookmark, making studying easier and more efficient.

- **LearningCurve adaptive quizzing and digital flash cards for review.** Students can access a gamelike LearningCurve quiz in each chapter to test their knowledge and reinforce learning of the material, and a digital flash cards feature gives students a new way to review key terms and concepts.

- **Video clips that extend and complement text content.** A rich library of LaunchPad videos offers easy access to clips from movies, TV shows, interviews, and more.

- **Media Literacy Activities.** Included in each chapter of LaunchPad, these activities encourage students to apply and practice their media literacy skills.

- **Practical career advice.** LaunchPad's career unit features video activities, relevant resources, and a thoroughly updated new edition of *Media Career Guide: Preparing for Jobs in the 21st Century*, Thirteenth Edition, which is packed with practical information for students who are considering a major in the media industries.

To learn more about LaunchPad for *Media & Culture* or to purchase access, go to **launchpadworks.com**.

Media Career Guide: Preparing for Jobs in the 21st Century, Thirteenth Edition

Practical, student-friendly, and revised to address recent trends in the job market, this guide includes a comprehensive directory of media jobs, useful tips, and career guidance for students who are considering a major in the media industries. *Media Career Guide* is available as an e-book, and it is also included on LaunchPad for *Media & Culture*.

The Essential Guide to Visual Communication

A concise introduction to the evolution, theory, and principles of visual communication in contemporary society, this guide helps students develop the skills they need to become critical consumers of visual media by examining images through the lens of visual rhetoric. Students see how images influence and persuade audiences, and how iconic images can be repurposed to communicate particular messages. *The Essential Guide to Visual Communication* can be packaged at a significant discount with the print book.

Instructor Resources

For more information or to order or download the instructor's resources, please visit the online catalog at **macmillanlearning.com/communication**. The Instructor's Resource Manual, test bank, lecture slides, and iClicker questions are also available on LaunchPad: **launchpadworks.com**.

LaunchPad for *Media & Culture*, Thirteenth Edition

At Bedford/St. Martin's, we are committed to providing online resources that meet the needs of instructors and students in powerful yet simple ways. We've taken what we've learned from both instructors and students to create a new generation of technology featuring LaunchPad. With its student-friendly approach, LaunchPad offers our trusted content—organized for easy assignability in a simple user interface.

- **An easy-to-use interface.** Ready-made interactive LaunchPad units give you the building blocks to assign instantly as is or to customize to fit your course. A unit's worth of work can be assigned in seconds, significantly decreasing the amount of time it takes for you to get your course up and running.

- **Intuitive and useful analytics.** The gradebook quickly and easily allows you to gauge performance for your whole class, for individual students, and for individual assignments, making class prep time as well as time spent with students more productive.

- **A fully interactive e-book.** Every LaunchPad e-book comes with powerful study tools, multimedia content, and easy customization options for instructors. Students can search, highlight, and bookmark, making studying easier and more efficient.
- **A wide range of activities, video, and other assignments.** In every chapter, students can tackle gamelike LearningCurve quizzes to test their knowledge and reinforce learning of the material, and new digital flash cards provide opportunities for review. In addition, a rich library of videos offers easy access to clips from movies, TV shows, interviews, and more, and Media Literacy Activities encourage students to apply and practice their media literacy skills. Finally, LaunchPad's career unit features video activities, relevant resources, and a thoroughly updated new edition of *Media Career Guide: Preparing for Jobs in the 21st Century*, Thirteenth Edition, which has been revised to address recent trends in the job market.
- **Instructor resources.** The Instructor's Resource Manual, test bank, lecture slides, and iClicker questions, as well as an assignable review quiz for each chapter, are all available on LaunchPad.

Instructor's Resource Manual

The best and most comprehensive instructor teaching tool available for introduction to mass communication courses provides a range of teaching approaches, tips for facilitating in-class discussions, writing assignments, outlines, lecture topics, lecture spin-offs, critical-process exercises, classroom media resources, and an annotated list of video resources. The Instructor's Resource Manual has gone interactive, with an assignable online media literacy activity for each chapter. These activities, adapted from and inspired by activities in the manual and built into each LaunchPad unit, provide students with extra practice as they develop their media literacy skills.

Test Bank

The *Media & Culture* test bank includes more than thirteen hundred questions, with multiple choice, true/false, and essay questions for every chapter. Feedback is also provided.

Lecture Slides

Lecture slide presentations help guide your lecture and are available for each chapter in the text.

iClicker Questions

iClicker question slides help keep your students engaged and help you make your class even more interactive. Now featuring more discussion-based content, these questions prompt engagement by encouraging students to participate, think critically, have fun, and get to know their instructors and peers. Questions can be used in class or asynchronously.

Acknowledgments

We are very grateful to everyone at Bedford/St. Martin's who supported this project through its many stages. We wish that every textbook author could have the kind of experience we have had with the Macmillan humanities team: Leasa Burton, Vice President of Humanities; Erika Gutierrez, Senior Program Director for Communication and College Success; Jane Knetzger, Director of Content Development; and so many others. Over the years, we have also collaborated with superb and supportive editors: on the thirteenth edition, Senior Development Editor Christina Lembo and Associate Editor Kathy McInerney. We particularly appreciate the tireless work of Ed Dionne, Senior Content Project Manager, who kept the book on schedule while making sure we got the details right, and Jennifer Wetzel, Senior Workflow Project Manager. Media is such an important part of this project, and our LaunchPad and media resources could not have come to fruition without our fantastic media team: Nicole Erazo, Media Editor, and Sarah O'Connor Kepes, Advanced Media Project Manager and Digital Activities Specialist. Thanks also to Executive Marketing Manager Scott Guile and his fearless marketing team, and to Billy Boardman for a fantastic cover design.

We also want to thank the many fine and thoughtful reviewers who contributed ideas over the years, including these reviewers who provided feedback for the thirteenth edition:

Stacy Barton, *Metropolitan State University of Denver*; Rachel Bornn, *Hudson Valley Community College*; Beth Butler, *Kent State University at Stark*; Kathryn D. Coduto, *South Dakota State University*; Samuel Ebersole, *Colorado State University Pueblo*; Betsy Emmons, *Samford University*; Tara M. Franks, *Sierra College*; Stacy Fitzpatrick, *North Hennepin Community College*; Lewis Freeman, *Fordham University*; Hilary Gamble, *Auburn University at Montgomery*; Carolyn Hardin, *Miami University of Ohio*; Paul Hillier, *University of Tampa*; Anthony J. Hoos, *Howard Community College*; Rachel Kerr, *Fredonia State University of New York*; Jodi Hallsten Lyczak, *Illinois State University*; Andrea Mason, *Arapahoe Community College*; Scott C. McHugh, *Kean University*; Rob McKenzie, *East Stroudsburg University of Pennsylvania*; Gigi McNamara, *University of Toledo*; Timothy C. Molina, *Northwest Vista College*; Eric Pierson, *University of San Diego*; Tim Posada, *Saddleback College*; Joshua Reeves, *Oregon State University and the University of Tyumen*; Margot Susca, *American University*; Yvette Walker, *University of Oklahoma–Norman*; and David Wolfgang, *Colorado State University–Fort Collins*.

Special thanks from Richard Campbell: I would also like to acknowledge the number of fine teachers at both the University of Wisconsin–Milwaukee and Northwestern University who helped shape the way I think about many of the issues raised in this book, and I am especially grateful to my former students at the University of Wisconsin–Milwaukee, Mount Mary College, the University of Michigan, Middle Tennessee State University, and Miami University. Some of my students have contributed directly to this text, and thousands have endured my courses over the years—and made them better. My all-time favorite former students, Chris Martin and Bettina Fabos, are coauthors of this text. I am grateful for Chris's and Bettina's fine writing, research savvy, good stories, and tireless work amid their own teaching schedules and writing careers, all while raising two spirited daughters. I also want to thank my good friend and Miami colleague Ron Becker, whose writing has added a much appreciated new voice to our textbook. A longtime *M&C* user, Ron is an outstanding teacher and distinguished media scholar. I remain most grateful, though, to the people I most love: my grandsons, Reese and Gus; my son, Chris; my daughter, Caitlin; and, most of all, my wife, Dianna, whose line editing, content ideas, daily conversations, shared interests, and ongoing support are the resources that make this project go smoother with each edition.

Special thanks from Christopher Martin and Bettina Fabos: We would also like to thank Richard Campbell, the founding author of this book project, who remains a great inspiration in thinking about media and culture. We also appreciate the great energy, creativity, and talent that everyone at Macmillan Learning brings to the book, especially Senior Developmental Editor Christina Lembo, whose tireless, thoughtful, thorough, and creative contributions have made this book project so rewarding. From edition to edition, we receive plenty of suggestions from *Media & Culture* users and reviewers and from our own journalism and media students. We would like to thank them for their input and for creating a community of sorts around the theme of critical perspectives on the media. Most of all, we'd like to thank our daughters, Olivia and Sabine, two young women who continue to bring us joy, laughter, and excellent media insights, as well as a sense of mission to better understand the world of media and culture in which they live.

Special thanks from Ron Becker: I can't thank my coauthors and everyone at Bedford/St. Martin's enough for inviting me to join the team. Getting the chance to work on a textbook after teaching with it (and admiring it) for fourteen years is an incredible privilege. Richard Campbell has been the most extraordinary mentor, and it has been a real pleasure to work with and learn from Christopher and Bettina. Christina Lembo's astute editorial guidance and saintlike patience were invaluable for me as a new author on the project. I would also like to thank several colleagues whose input is evident throughout, including Mack Hagood, Elana Levine, Jason Mittel, Michael Newman, Carolyn Hardin, Matthew Crain, Denise McCoskey, Taylor Cole Miller, Jennifer Fuller, Julie D'Acci, John Fiske, and Michele Hilmes. I would also like to thank the undergraduate assistants whom I have the honor of working with each year; their energy and insights feed my passion for the topic. Most of all, I'd like to thank my husband, Marc, whose work ethic humbles me and whose knowledge about digital technologies was invaluable to this project in so many ways.

Media & Culture, Thirteenth Edition, Connects to the Learning Outcomes of the National Communication Association

The National Communication Association has published learning outcomes for courses within the discipline. The following table shows how these learning outcomes are reflected in *Media & Culture*, Thirteenth Edition.

Learning Outcome	Campbell, *Media & Culture*, 13th Edition
Employ communication theories, perspectives, principles, and concepts	**Chapter 1: Media, Culture, and Communication: A Critical Approach** gives students a solid overview of media communication. • **"How We Got Here: Culture, Technology, and the Evolution of Media Communication"** explores the relationship among culture, technology, and media and provides an introduction to media communication through the years, moving from the oral and written eras to the print revolution, through the electronic era, and into the digital era. • **"Media in Our Digital Era"** plants the seeds of convergence and its effects on business and culture; discusses the power and ubiquity of the media environment that surrounds us; and explores the viewing practices, participation, and fragmentation that characterize media culture in our digital era. • **"Thinking Differently about Media and Culture"** introduces accessible models students can employ to reflect on the meaning, impact, and importance of media use—in their own lives and in our society as a whole. **Chapter 15: Media Effects and Cultural Approaches to Research** is directly focused on these learning outcomes and examines specific mass communication theories and both social scientific and cultural studies research perspectives. **Industry-specific chapters** throughout the book provide in-depth study and exploration of the types of mass communication: • Chapter 2: The Internet and Digital Media • Chapter 3: Digital Gaming and the Media Playground • Chapter 4: Sound Recording and Popular Music • Chapter 5: Popular Radio and the Origins of Broadcasting • Chapter 6: Television: From Broadcasting to Streaming • Chapter 7: Movies and the Power of Images • Chapter 8: Newspapers: The Rise and Decline of Modern Journalism • Chapter 9: Magazines in the Age of Specialization • Chapter 10: Books and the Power of Print The **history of mass media** is threaded throughout the book. Book sections that specifically explore history include the following: • "How We Got Here: Culture, Technology, and the Evolution of Media Communication" and "Historical Perspective: Connecting the Past to the Present" in Chapter 1 • "How We Got Here: The Development of the Internet" in Chapter 2 • "How We Got Here: The Development of Digital Gaming" in Chapter 3 • "How We Got Here: The Development of Sound Recording" in Chapter 4 • "How We Got Here: The Development of Radio," "The Evolution of U.S. Radio," and "Radio Reinvents Itself" in Chapter 5 • "How We Got Here: The Birth of Broadcast TV," "The Network Era: The Big Three Dominate TV," and "The Post-Network Era: Competition Heats Up" in Chapter 6 • "How We Got Here: The Early Development of Movies," "The Rise and Decline of Hollywood's Studio System Era," and "Hollywood and Movies after the Studio System Era" in Chapter 7 • "How We Got Here: The Early Development of American Newspapers" and "Competing Models of Modern Newspaper Journalism" in Chapter 8 • "How We Got Here: The Early History of Magazines" and "The Arrival of Mass-Circulation National Magazines" in Chapter 9 • "How We Got Here: The Early History of Books" and "Mass Publishing and the Book Industry" in Chapter 10 • "How We Got Here: The Development of American Advertising" in Chapter 11 • "How We Got Here: Early Developments in Public Relations" in Chapter 12 • "How We Got Here: The Rise of Global Conglomerates" in Chapter 13 • "How We Got Here: The Evolution of American Journalism" in Chapter 14 • "How We Got Here: Early Types of Media Research" in Chapter 15 • "How We Got Here: The Origins of Free Expression and a Free Press" in Chapter 16 **LaunchPad video activities** in each chapter give students the opportunity to hear from industry professionals, make connections with film and TV clips, and explore current issues in media.

Learning Outcome	Campbell, *Media & Culture*, 13th Edition
Engage in communication inquiry	**Media Literacy and the Critical Process** boxes in each chapter provide real-life examples of how we interact with the media, and a step-by-step breakdown of the critical process helps students practice the art of critical thinking. **LaunchPad** provides an additional interactive and assignable Media Literacy Activity for each chapter, which allows students to practice their skills as critical consumers of the media. Even more Media Literacy Activities in the **Instructor's Resource Manual** provide instructors with ideas for additional practice that they can use as classroom activities or as inspiration for assignments.
Critically analyze messages	*Media & Culture's* critical and cultural approach to the media, particularly the five-step **Media Literacy and the Critical Process** boxes, gets students describing, examining, analyzing, interpreting, evaluating, and engaging in topics in the media to actively build media literacy. Assignable **Media Literacy Activities on LaunchPad** allow students to practice their skills as critical consumers of the media. Even more Media Literacy Activities in the **Instructor's Resource Manual** provide instructors with ideas for additional practice that they can use as classroom activities or as inspiration for assignments. The thirteenth edition's new **Case Study: A Guide to Identifying Fake News**—an extension of the critical process activities that students have done throughout the term—prompts students to further develop their media literacy and critical-thinking skills by learning more about disinformation and analyzing the credibility of contemporary media stories.
Demonstrate the ability to accomplish communicative goals (self-efficacy)	A **career unit** on LaunchPad helps students on the path toward exploring and realizing their future career goals. This unit includes the latest edition of the ***Media Career Guide***, which is full of tips and information that students can use to help define and achieve their career goals in the communication fields of their choice. Additionally, the **Media Literacy and the Critical Process** boxes and activities allow students the space to practice and develop their skills as critical consumers of the media.
Apply ethical communication principles and practices	*Media & Culture* strives to help students understand contemporary issues and controversies. The **Examining Ethics** boxes in particular dig deep into exploring such issues and controversies. These boxes discuss ethics issues across the media industries: • "Telling Stories about 'Voices We Seldom Hear" in Chapter 1 • "Algorithmic Bias" in Chapter 2 • "The Gender Problem in Digital Games" in Chapter 3 • "YouTube: How One of the Richest Companies Shortchanges Music Artists" in Chapter 4 • "How Did Talk Radio Become So One-Sided?" in Chapter 5 • "Is This Entertainment? TV Industry Reconsiders Police Shows" in Chapter 6 • "Breaking through Hollywood's Race Barrier" in Chapter 7 • "The 1619 Project—Journalism Takes the Long View to Rethink History" in Chapter 8 • "The Evolution of Photojournalism" in Chapter 9 • "Banned Books: Controversial Because They Are Real" in Chapter 10 • "Do Alcohol Ads Encourage Binge Drinking?" in Chapter 11 • "Egg on The North Face—a Wikipedia Scandal" in Chapter 12 • "Are the Big Digital Companies Too Big?" in Chapter 13 • "Black Journalists Lead an 'Overdue Reckoning' on Objectivity" in Chapter 14 • "Our Masculinity Problem" in Chapter 15 • "Is 'Sexting' Pornography?" in Chapter 16 The new **Case Study: A Guide to Identifying Fake News** examines the history, definition, and typology of misinformation in our current media environment. Carefully crafted to spotlight useful source standards, the guide incorporates the critical process and includes a survey activity that students can use to assess the credibility of a story for themselves. **Chapter 14: The Culture of Journalism: Values, Ethics, and Democracy** digs into the ethics issues and judgment calls that journalists face every day. The chapter also explores the values that journalists promise to uphold. **Chapter 15: Media Effects and Cultural Approaches to Research** provides an in-depth study of media's impact on society, taking students through early types of media research, research on media effects, cultural approaches to media research, and media research and democracy. **Media Literacy and the Critical Process** boxes and interactive online activities help students hone their critical media skills.

Learning Outcome	Campbell, *Media & Culture*, 13th Edition
Utilize communication to embrace difference	Content throughout the book explores the connection between communication and culture and incorporates a range of diverse perspectives and discussions. In particular, the **Global Village** boxes connect students with issues from all over the world: • "Social Media Fraud and Elections" in Chapter 2 • "Phones in Hand, the World Finds Pokémon" in Chapter 3 • "Aya Nakamura: France's Global Pop Star" in Chapter 4 • "Radio Stories from Around the World" in Chapter 5 • "Telling and Selling Stories around the World" in Chapter 6 • "Beyond Hollywood: Asian Cinema" in Chapter 7 • "The World's Biggest Newspapers" in Chapter 8 • "Cosmopolitan Style Travels the World" in Chapter 9 • "Buenos Aires, the World's Bookstore Capital" in Chapter 10 • "The Unfairness of Fairness Creams" in Chapter 11 • "Public Relations and Bananas" in Chapter 12 • "China's Dominant Media Corporations Rival America's" in Chapter 13 • "Authoritarians Use 'Fake News' Allegations as a Weapon" in Chapter 14 • "International Media Research" in Chapter 15 • "The Challenges of Film Censorship in China" in Chapter 16 **"The Politics of Media Representations"** section in Chapter 1 also prompts students to consider how media representations reflect and contribute to the distribution of power, status, resources, and visibility in a culture, and emphasizes the importance of interrogating these media representations in terms of fairness and equity. These **issues are further explored** in later chapters, with discussions that include gender and racial diversity in digital gaming (Chapter 3), gay material and the quality audience during television's post-network era (Chapter 6), and how journalistic objectivity and newsroom diversity are being reconsidered in light of the racial justice movement (Chapters 8 and 14).
Influence public discourse	The relationship among **politics, democracy, and the media** is a recurring theme in *Media & Culture*. Examples can be found throughout, including: • "Three Roles: Media Consumer, Media Producer, and Media Citizen" in Chapter 1 • "The Internet, Digital Communication, and Democracy" in Chapter 2 • "Digital Gaming, Free Speech, and Democracy" in Chapter 3 • "Sound Recording, Breaking Barriers, and Democracy" in Chapter 4 • "Radio and the Democracy of the Airwaves" in Chapter 5 • "Television and Democracy" in Chapter 6 • "Popular Movies and Democracy" in Chapter 7 • "Newspapers and Democracy" in Chapter 8 • "Magazines in a Democratic Society" in Chapter 9 • "Books and the Future of Democracy" in Chapter 10 • "Advertising, Politics, and Democracy" in Chapter 11 • "Public Relations and Democracy" in Chapter 12 • "The Media Marketplace and Democracy" in Chapter 13 • "Journalism's Role in Democracy" in Chapter 14 • "Media Research and Democracy" in Chapter 15 • "The First Amendment and Democracy" in Chapter 16 **Chapter 16: Legal Controls and Freedom of Expression** takes a close look at the First Amendment and how it relates to mass media. Finally, the last step of the critical process discussed throughout the text is **engagement**, which urges students to become involved in the public discourse surrounding media questions of the day.

Contents

ABOUT THE AUTHORS *vii*
BRIEF CONTENTS *viii*
PREFACE *ix*

**1 Media, Culture, and Communication:
A Critical Approach *3***

Understanding the Media Today *4*

**How We Got Here: Culture, Technology, and the Evolution of Media
Communication** *5*

Oral and Written Eras in Communication *7*

The Print Era *7*

The Electronic Era *8*

The Digital Revolution *10*

Media in Our Digital Era *10*

Convergence *10*

Media Culture in the Digital Era *11*

The Media Environment in Our Digital Era *12*

Thinking Differently about Media and Culture *14*

Three Roles: Media Consumer, Media Producer, and Media Citizen *14*

Historical Perspective: Connecting the Past to the Present *15*

The Linear Model of Mass Communication *16*

A Cultural Approach to Media and Communication *16*

▶ **LaunchPad** *Black Panther* on Film *17*

Media and the Politics of Culture *19*

Media and Representation *19*

▶ **LaunchPad** Agenda-Setting and Gatekeeping *20*

The Politics of Evaluating the Media *20*

◼ **EXAMINING ETHICS** Telling Stories about "Voices We Seldom Hear" *22*

Media Literacy in Action: The Critical Process *26*

The Five Steps of the Critical Process *26*

Benefits of a Critical Perspective *27*

◼ **MEDIA LITERACY & THE CRITICAL PROCESS** *28*

CHAPTER REVIEW *30*

▶ **LaunchPad** *30*

Mario Tama/Getty Images

▶ **For videos, review quizzing, and more, visit LaunchPad for *Media & Culture* at launchpadworks.com.**

Ｍ LaunchPad

Ron Becker

2 The Internet and Digital Media *33*

The Internet Today *34*

How We Got Here: The Development of the Internet *35*

  The Pre-Web Internet *35*

  Web 1.0: The Internet Becomes a Mass Medium *37*

  Web 2.0: The Internet Gets Interactive *38*

  Web 3.0: The Internet Starts to Think *39*

  ▣ **EXAMINING ETHICS** Algorithmic Bias 40

Our Complex Digital Environment *41*

  Decentralizing the Creation and Spread of Information *41*

  Building Online Communities *42*

  ▣ **GLOBAL VILLAGE** Social Media Fraud and Elections 43

  Manipulating Media *45*

The Business of Controlling the Internet *47*

  Controlling Data *47*

  ▣ **MEDIA LITERACY & THE CRITICAL PROCESS** Harnessing Creativity by Stepping Away from Your Phone 48

  Controlling Access *50*

  ▶ **LaunchPad** Net Neutrality *51*

  Regaining Control *52*

The Internet, Digital Communication, and Democracy *54*

CHAPTER REVIEW *56*

  ▶ **LaunchPad** *56*

3   Digital Gaming and the Media Playground   *59*

Digital Gaming Today   *60*

How We Got Here: The Development of Digital Gaming   *61*

    Mechanical Gaming   *62*

    The First Video Games   *62*

    Consoles and Advancing Graphics   *64*

    Gaming on PCs   *66*

    Mobile Gaming   *66*

The Gaming Environment   *67*

    Video Game Genres   *68*

    Social Gaming   *69*

    Players: Inside the Game   *70*

Communities of Play   *71*

    Collective Intelligence   *71*

    Interactive Livestreaming Platforms: Gaming Becomes Television   *71*

    ▣ **GLOBAL VILLAGE** Phones in Hand, the World Finds Pokémon   *72*

    Fantasy Sports   *74*

    Conventions   *74*

Digital Gaming and Society   *75*

    Digital Gaming and Media Culture   *75*

    ⊙ **LaunchPad** Video Games at the Movies   *76*

    Addiction and Other Concerns   *76*

    ⊙ **LaunchPad** Portrayals of Women in Video Games   *77*

    ▣ **EXAMINING ETHICS** The Gender Problem in Digital Games   *78*

    ▣ **MEDIA LITERACY & THE CRITICAL PROCESS** First-Person Shooter Games: Misogyny as Entertainment?   *80*

    The Future of Gaming and Interactive Environments   *81*

The Business of Digital Gaming   *81*

    The Ownership of Digital Game Publishing   *82*

    The Structure of Digital Game Publishing   *83*

    Selling Digital Games   *84*

    Digital Gaming and Advertising   *85*

Digital Gaming, Free Speech, and Democracy   *85*

CHAPTER REVIEW   *88*

    ⊙ **LaunchPad**   *88*

Kazuhiro NOGI/AFP/Getty Images

Paras Griffin/Getty Images

4 Sound Recording and Popular Music *91*

Sound Recording Today *92*

How We Got Here: The Development of Sound Recording *93*

From Cylinders to Disks: Sound Recording Becomes a Mass Medium *94*

▶ **LaunchPad** Sound Recordings from a Century Ago *95*

From Audiotape to CDs: Analog Goes Digital *96*

Sound Recording in the Internet Age *97*

▶ **LaunchPad** Recording Music Today *97*

The Ongoing Battles between Records and Radio *98*

The Culture of Popular Music *99*

The Rise of Pop Music *99*

Rock and Roll Is Here to Stay *100*

Rock Muddies the Waters *101*

Pushback against Early Rock and Roll *103*

Popular Music's Continuing Reinvention *105*

The British Are Coming! *105*

Motor City Music: Detroit Gives America Soul *106*

Folk and Psychedelic Music Reflect the Times *107*

▣ **MEDIA LITERACY & THE CRITICAL PROCESS** Music Preferences across Generations *108*

Punk and Indie Respond to Mainstream Rock *109*

Hip-Hop Redraws Musical Lines *110*

Pop in the Age of Music Fragmentation *111*

▣ **GLOBAL VILLAGE** Aya Nakamura: France's Global Pop Star *112*

The Business of Sound Recording *113*

Global Music Corporations Influence the Industry *113*

Making, Selling, and Profiting from Music *114*

Sound Recording, Breaking Barriers, and Democracy *116*

▣ **EXAMINING ETHICS** YouTube: How One of the Richest Companies Shortchanges Music Artists *118*

CHAPTER REVIEW *120*

▶ **LaunchPad** *120*

5   Popular Radio and the Origins of Broadcasting   *123*

Radio Today   *124*

How We Got Here: The Early Development of Radio   *125*

The Discovery of Radio Waves   *125*

The Inventors of Wireless Telegraphy   *126*

Wireless Telephony: Radio Gets a Voice   *127*

Regulating and Controlling a New Medium   *128*

The Evolution of U.S. Radio   *130*

AT&T's Power Grab: The First Radio Ads and the First Radio Network   *131*

RCA's Era of Dominating Radio   *132*

CBS: NBC Gets a Strong Rival   *134*

Bringing Order to Chaos with Additional Regulation   *134*

The Golden Age of Radio   *135*

Radio Reinvents Itself   *138*

Transistors Make Radio Portable   *138*

The FM Revolution and Edwin Armstrong   *139*

The Rise of Format and Top 40 Radio   *140*

Resisting the Top 40   *141*

The Sounds of the Contemporary Radio Environment   *141*

Format Specialization   *141*

▣ EXAMINING ETHICS How Did Talk Radio Become So One-Sided?   *143*

Nonprofit Radio and NPR   *144*

Radio beyond Broadcasting   *145*

▣ MEDIA LITERACY & THE CRITICAL PROCESS Comparing Commercial and Noncommercial Radio   *146*

▶ LaunchPad Radio: Yesterday, Today, and Tomorrow   *147*

▣ GLOBAL VILLAGE Radio Stories from around the World   *148*

The Economics of Radio   *150*

Local and National Advertising   *150*

Manipulating Playlists with Payola   *150*

Broadcast Radio Ownership: From Diversity to Consolidation   *151*

Radio and the Democracy of the Airwaves   *152*

CHAPTER REVIEW   *154*

▶ LaunchPad   *154*

Heather Kennedy/Getty Images

©Netflix/Everett Collection, Inc

6 Television: From Broadcasting to Streaming 157

Television Today 158

How We Got Here: The Birth of Broadcast TV 159

Inventing Visual Radio 160

Making TV Ready for the Masses 160

The Broadcast Model Defines Early TV 161

How Should It Look? Making TV Programs 163

The Network Era: The Big Three Dominate TV 165

The Networks Take Control of Programming 165

Programming for Profits 166

"A Vast Wasteland" 169

▶ **LaunchPad** What Makes Public Television Public? 170

The Post-Network Era: Competition Heats Up 171

Pay for TV? Cable Brings the Subscription Model 171

Competition beyond Cable 173

Programming Strategies in the Post-Network Era 174

▣ **EXAMINING ETHICS** Is This Entertainment? TV Industry Reconsiders Police Shows 177

▣ **MEDIA LITERACY & THE CRITICAL PROCESS** TV and the State of Storytelling 178

Our Digital Era and the Business of TV 178

The Infrastructure of Digital TV 179

Watching TV in the Digital Era 180

The Economics of Delivering Content to Viewers 181

Making Digital TV Content 184

▣ **GLOBAL VILLAGE** Telling and Selling Stories around the World 186

Television Ownership 187

Television and Democracy 188

CHAPTER REVIEW 190

▶ **LaunchPad** 190

7 Movies and the Power of Images *193*

⊳ **LaunchPad** Storytelling in *Star Wars* *194*

Movies Today *194*

How We Got Here: The Early Development of Movies *195*

The Development of Film Technology *196*

The Introduction of Narrative in the Silent Era *198*

The Arrival of Nickelodeons *199*

The First Movie Cartel *199*

The Rise and Decline of Hollywood's Studio System Era *200*

How the Studio System Worked *200*

Classical Hollywood Cinema Style *202*

The Decline of the Studio System and Hollywood's Golden Age *204*

Hollywood and Movies after the Studio System Era *207*

Major Studios Evolve *207*

Directors as Movie "Authors" *207*

Movies Outside Hollywood *209*

▣ **EXAMINING ETHICS** Breaking through Hollywood's Race Barrier *210*

▣ **GLOBAL VILLAGE** Beyond Hollywood: Asian Cinema *212*

The Economics of the Movie Business *215*

The Major Studios *216*

Making Money on Movies Today *217*

▣ **MEDIA LITERACY & THE CRITICAL PROCESS** The Blockbuster Mentality *219*

Popular Movies and Democracy *221*

⊳ **LaunchPad** More Than a Movie: Social Issues and Film *221*

CHAPTER REVIEW *222*

⊳ **LaunchPad** *222*

© Lucasfilm Ltd./Everett Collection, Inc

Joe Amon/The Denver Post/Getty Images

8 Newspapers: The Rise and Decline of Modern Journalism *225*

Newspapers Today *226*

How We Got Here: The Early Development of American Newspapers *227*

Colonial Newspapers and the Partisan Press *227*

The Penny Press Era: Newspapers Become Mass Media *228*

The Age of Yellow Journalism: Sensationalism and Investigation *230*

Competing Models of Modern Newspaper Journalism *232*

The Rise of "Objectivity" in Modern Journalism *232*

Interpretive Journalism *233*

Literary Forms of Journalism *235*

Newspapers in the TV and Internet Age *236*

The Business, Organization, and Ownership of Newspapers *237*

Consensus versus Conflict: Newspapers Play Different Roles *237*

▣ **EXAMINING ETHICS** The 1619 Project—Journalism Takes the Long View to Rethink History *238*

Newspapers beyond the Mainstream *240*

Newspaper Operations *243*

▣ **MEDIA LITERACY & THE CRITICAL PROCESS** Covering the Unionization of Newspaper Workers *245*

Newspaper Ownership: Investment Companies Dominate the Industry *246*

Challenges and Changes Facing Newspapers Today *247*

Declines in Readership, Newsrooms, and Newspapers *247*

▶ **LaunchPad** Community Voices: Weekly Newspapers *248*

▣ **GLOBAL VILLAGE** The World's Biggest Newspapers *249*

Searching for Success in the Digital Era *250*

New Models for Newspapers *251*

Newspapers and Democracy *253*

CHAPTER REVIEW *254*

▶ **LaunchPad** *254*

9 Magazines in the Age of Specialization *257*

Magazines Today *258*

How We Got Here: The Early History of Magazines *259*

Early British Magazines *259*

Magazines in Colonial America *259*

U.S. Magazines and Specialization *260*

General Interest, Women's, and Illustrated Magazines *261*

The Arrival of Mass-Circulation National Magazines *262*

Social Reform and the Muckrakers *262*

The Era of General-Interest Magazines *263*

▣ **EXAMINING ETHICS** The Evolution of Photojournalism *264*

The Fall of General-Interest Magazines *267*

The Domination of Specialization *269*

▶ **LaunchPad** Magazine Specialization Today *269*

Men's and Women's Magazines *269*

Entertainment, Sports, and Leisure Magazines *270*

▣ **GLOBAL VILLAGE** Cosmopolitan Style Travels the World *271*

Magazines for the Ages *272*

Elite Magazines *272*

▣ **MEDIA LITERACY & THE CRITICAL PROCESS** Uncovering American Beauty *273*

Magazines Targeting Race, Ethnicity, and Sexuality *273*

Supermarket Tabloids *274*

The Organization and Economics of Magazines *275*

▶ **LaunchPad** Narrowcasting in Magazines *275*

Inside Magazines: Creating Branded Content *275*

Departments and Duties *276*

Major Magazine Chains *278*

Independently Owned Magazines *278*

Magazines in a Democratic Society *279*

CHAPTER REVIEW *280*

▶ **LaunchPad** *280*

Rob Kim/Getty Images

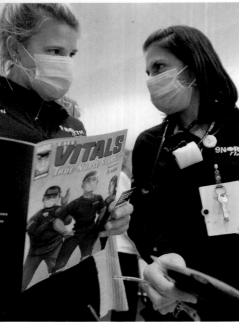

Greg Wohlford/USA TODAY NETWORK

10 Books and the Power of Print 283

Books Today 284

How We Got Here: The Early History of Books 285

The Development of Manuscript Culture 286

The Innovations of Block Printing and Movable Type 286

The Gutenberg Revolution: The Invention of the Printing Press 287

The Birth of Publishing in the United States 287

Mass Publishing and the Book Industry 288

The Formation of Publishing Houses 288

Types of Books 289

Trends and Issues in Book Publishing 292

Influences of Television and Film 292

▶ **LaunchPad** Based On: Making Books into Movies 293

E-Books 293

Audio Books 293

Preserving and Digitizing Books 294

Censorship and Banned Books 294

▣ **EXAMINING ETHICS** Banned Books: Controversial Because They Are Real 295

The Organization and Economics of the Book Industry 296

Ownership Patterns 297

The Structure of Book Publishing 298

▣ **MEDIA LITERACY & THE CRITICAL PROCESS** Publishing Gatekeepers: Who Gets to Write the Big Books? 300

Selling Books: Book Superstores and Independent Booksellers 300

▶ **LaunchPad** Amazon's Brick-and-Mortar Bookstores 301

Selling Books Online 302

▣ **GLOBAL VILLAGE** Buenos Aires, the World's Bookstore Capital 303

Self-Published Books 304

Books and the Future of Democracy 305

CHAPTER REVIEW 306

▶ **LaunchPad** 306

11 Advertising and Commercial Culture *309*

Advertising Today *310*

How We Got Here: The Development of American Advertising *311*

The First Advertising Agencies *312*

Advertising in the 1800s *312*

Promoting Social Change and Dictating Values *314*

Early Ad Regulation *315*

The Influence of Visual Design *315*

The Shape of Contemporary U.S. Advertising *316*

Types of Advertising Agencies *316*

The Structure of Ad Agencies *318*

Trends in Online Advertising *320*

Persuasive Techniques in Contemporary Advertising *324*

Conventional Persuasive Strategies *324*

The Association Principle *325*

Advertising as Myth and Story *326*

▣ **MEDIA LITERACY & THE CRITICAL PROCESS** The Branded You *327*

Product Placement *327*

Advertising and Concerns about Commercial Speech *328*

Critical Issues in Advertising *329*

▶ **LaunchPad** Advertising and Effects on Children *329*

▣ **EXAMINING ETHICS** Do Alcohol Ads Encourage Binge Drinking? *332*

▣ **GLOBAL VILLAGE** The Unfairness of Fairness Creams *334*

Watching Over Advertising *336*

Advertising, Politics, and Democracy *338*

Advertising's Role in Politics *338*

The Future of Advertising *339*

CHAPTER REVIEW *340*

▶ **LaunchPad** *340*

Jon Kopaloff/Getty Images

Materials developed by CDC

12 Public Relations and Framing the Message 343

Public Relations Today 344

How We Got Here: Early Developments in Public Relations 346
The First Publicists and Press Agents: P. T. Barnum and Buffalo Bill 346
Helping Big Business 347
The Birth of Modern Public Relations 347

The Practice of Public Relations 350
The Business of Public Relations 350
Performing Public Relations 351
▣ EXAMINING ETHICS Egg on The North Face—a Wikipedia Scandal 354
▣ GLOBAL VILLAGE Public Relations and Bananas 356

Tensions between Public Relations and the Press 359
▶ LaunchPad Give and Take: Public Relations and Journalism 359
Elements of Professional Friction 360
▣ MEDIA LITERACY & THE CRITICAL PROCESS The Invisible Hand of PR 361
Shaping the Image of Public Relations 362

Public Relations and Democracy 363

CHAPTER REVIEW 364
▶ LaunchPad 364

13 Media Economics and the Global Marketplace *367*

Media Economics Today *368*

How We Got Here: The Rise of Global Conglomerates *370*

The Changing Role of Regulation *370*

Globalization Expands Media Markets *373*

The Internet and Digital Convergence *374*

◼ **EXAMINING ETHICS** Are the Big Digital Companies Too Big? *375*

◼ **GLOBAL VILLAGE** China's Dominant Media Corporations Rival America's *377*

Media Powerhouses and the Consolidation Frenzy *378*

Business Trends in Today's Media Industries *378*

Making Money from Media Products *379*

The Rise of Specialization *379*

Horizontal Integration and Synergy *380*

Vertical Integration *381*

Disney: A Twenty-First Century Media Conglomerate *381*

▶ **LaunchPad** Disney's Global Brand *381*

Social and Political Issues in Media Economics *384*

Conflicts over Conglomeration *386*

▶ **LaunchPad** The Impact of Media Ownership *386*

Employment Issues *387*

Belief in the Free Market *388*

Cultural Politics and Global Media *391*

◼ **MEDIA LITERACY & THE CRITICAL PROCESS** Cultural Imperialism and Movies *392*

The Media Marketplace and Democracy *393*

The Effects of Media Consolidation on Democracy *393*

The Media Reform Movement *394*

CHAPTER REVIEW *396*

▶ **LaunchPad** *396*

Presley Ann/Getty Images

AP Photo/Jose Luis Magana

14 The Culture of Journalism: Values, Ethics, and Democracy *399*

Journalism Today *400*

How We Got Here: The Evolution of American Journalism *401*

The Historical Foundations of Print Journalism *402*

Stories Become Visual on TV News *403*

Cable TV Pundits and Politics *405*

▶ LaunchPad The Contemporary Journalist: Pundit or Reporter? *406*

News Now: The Loss of Traditional Gatekeepers *406*

The Essential Elements of News *407*

What Is News? *407*

Characteristics of News *408*

▣ GLOBAL VILLAGE Authoritarians Use "Fake News" Allegations as a Weapon *409*

Values in American Journalism *410*

Ethics and the News Media *411*

Ethical Predicaments *411*

Resolving Ethical Problems *414*

Reporting Rituals and the Legacy of Print Journalism *415*

Focusing on the Present *415*

▣ MEDIA LITERACY & THE CRITICAL PROCESS Telling Stories and Covering Disaster *416*

Relying on Experts *417*

Balancing Story Conflict *418*

Acting as Adversaries *419*

The Rise of Conservative Media and the Idea of "Fake News" *419*

The Origins of Conservative Media *420*

Stoking White Working-Class Grievances *422*

Allegations of "Fake News" *422*

Journalism's Role in Democracy *423*

▣ EXAMINING ETHICS Black Journalists Lead an "Overdue Reckoning" on Objectivity *424*

Social Responsibility *425*

Making the Eagle Fly *425*

CHAPTER REVIEW *426*

▶ LaunchPad *426*

15 Media Effects and Cultural Approaches to Research *429*

▶ **LaunchPad** Suicide on TV *430*

Research on Media Today *430*

How We Got Here: Early Types of Media Research *431*

Propaganda Analysis *432*

Public Opinion Research *432*

Social Psychology Studies *433*

Marketing Research *433*

Research on Media Effects *434*

▣ **MEDIA LITERACY & THE CRITICAL PROCESS** Wedding Media and the Meaning of the Perfect Wedding Day *435*

Early Theories of Media Effects *435*

Conducting Media Effects Research *437*

▶ **LaunchPad** Media Effects Research *439*

Today's Leading Media Effects Theories *439*

▣ **EXAMINING ETHICS** Our Masculinity Problem *442*

Evaluating Research on Media Effects *442*

▶ **LaunchPad** Masculinity on Screen *443*

Cultural Approaches to Media Research *444*

Early Developments in Cultural Studies Research *444*

Conducting Cultural Studies Research *444*

▣ **GLOBAL VILLAGE** International Media Research *446*

Cultural Studies' Theoretical Perspectives *448*

Evaluating Cultural Studies Research *449*

Media Research and Democracy *450*

CHAPTER REVIEW *452*

▶ **LaunchPad** *452*

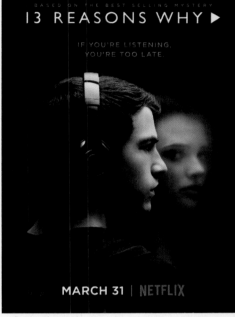

BASED ON THE BEST SELLING MYSTERY

13 REASONS WHY ▶

IF YOU'RE LISTENING,
YOU'RE TOO LATE.

MARCH 31 | NETFLIX

Netflix/Photofest

Alex Wong/Getty Images News/Getty Images

**16 Legal Controls and Freedom
of Expression** *455*

Free Expression Today *456*

How We Got Here: The Origins of Free Expression and a Free Press *458*

Freedom of Expression around the World *458*

The First Amendment of the U.S. Constitution *459*

The Limits to Freedom of Expression in the United States *460*

Censorship as Prior Restraint *460*

▣ **MEDIA LITERACY & THE CRITICAL PROCESS** Who Knows the First
Amendment? *462*

Unprotected Forms of Expression *463*

▣ **EXAMINING ETHICS** Is "Sexting" Pornography? *468*

▶ **LaunchPad** Sexting and Obscenity *468*

First Amendment versus Sixth Amendment *470*

Film and the First Amendment *472*

Social and Political Pressures on the Movies *472*

Early Self-Regulation in the Movie Industry *473*

The MPAA Rating System *474*

▣ **GLOBAL VILLAGE** The Challenges of Film Censorship in China *475*

Expression in the Media: Print, Broadcast, and Online *476*

The FCC Regulates Broadcasting *477*

Dirty Words, Indecent Speech, and Hefty Fines *477*

Political Broadcasts and Equal Opportunity *478*

The Demise of the Fairness Doctrine *479*

Communication Policy and the Internet *479*

▶ **LaunchPad** Bloggers and Legal Rights *481*

The First Amendment and Democracy *481*

CHAPTER REVIEW *482*

▶ **LaunchPad** *482*

CASE STUDY:
A GUIDE TO IDENTIFYING FAKE NEWS *485*

Defining Fake News *487*

Types of Fake News *488*

    Satirists *488*

    Hoaxes and Hucksters *488*

    Opinion Entrepreneurs *489*

    Propagandists *489*

    Information Anarchists *490*

The Critical Process: Identifying Fake News *491*

    Description *491*

    Analysis *491*

    Interpretation *493*

    Evaluation *494*

    Engagement *494*

NOTES *N-1*

GLOSSARY *G-1*

INDEX *I-1*

MEDIA & CULTURE

Media, Culture, and Communication

A CRITICAL APPROACH

The year 2020 was perhaps the most seismic year in a generation, or maybe even in a century or more. With the COVID-19 pandemic, the worst economy since the Great Depression, a national protest movement for social justice that reverberated around the world, and the most divisive national political climate in memory, capped off by a presidential election and its tumultuous aftermath—it was hard to make sense of a year that overflowed with such news.

Even before the worst of 2020 hit, people were already struggling with information overload. A Gallup/Knight poll of Americans (taken just before the pandemic and social justice movements hit the United States) found that "Americans feel overwhelmed by the volume and speed of news."[1]

Media outlets tried to help people put the year in historical perspective, by comparing it first to 1918, the year of another global pandemic, and then to other significant moments in time, including 1929 (the year of the economic crash that started the Great Depression), 1968 (a year of political chaos and protests for racial justice), 1919 and 1943 (years of other clashes for racial justice), 1941 (the shocking attack on Pearl Harbor), 1868 (when President Andrew Johnson, Lincoln's successor, undermined Black civil liberties), and—perhaps the scariest comparison—the period from 1347 to 1351, when the Black Death killed roughly half of Europe's population.

These global mega-stories conjuring historical comparisons weren't even all of the year's significant news. Other stories included the extraordinary wildfires scorching Australia and the western United States, the impeachment and acquittal of President Donald Trump, the death of basketball superstar Kobe Bryant and others in a helicopter crash, the United Kingdom's withdrawal from the European Union, the meltdown of the presidential nominating process at the Iowa caucus, and the long, drawn-out count of a record number of ballots for president in November.

Many Americans responded to 2020 with a sense of dread (panic-buying toilet paper), escapism (binge-watching *Tiger King* on Netflix, creating short dance videos on TikTok), activism (taking to

◀ In May 2020, a cell phone video showing a white Minneapolis police officer with his knee on the neck of George Floyd, a Black man, as Floyd repeatedly said he couldn't breathe, reignited protests for racial justice around the world—including here, on Hollywood Boulevard in Los Angeles.

UNDERSTANDING THE
MEDIA TODAY
p. 4

HOW WE GOT
HERE: CULTURE,
TECHNOLOGY, AND
THE EVOLUTION
OF MEDIA
COMMUNICATION
p. 5

MEDIA IN OUR
DIGITAL ERA
p. 10

THINKING
DIFFERENTLY ABOUT
MEDIA AND CULTURE
p. 14

MEDIA AND THE
POLITICS OF CULTURE
p. 19

MEDIA LITERACY IN
ACTION: THE CRITICAL
PROCESS
p. 26

the streets in #BlackLivesMatter protests across the country), and increased media communication, reaching out to others while still trying to "be safe," as the common greeting urged.

In fact, it was people's own communications that likely sustained them during this time. Dark humor flowed through social media memes, like the image of a swing set built so close to a brick wall that anyone attempting to swing would crash into it (caption: "If 2020 was a swing") and a still shot of late infomercial pitchman Billy Mays shouting "But wait, there's more" to illustrate that some new horror always seemed just around the corner (caption: "2020 every second"). A singing trio named Avenue Beat posted a song called "F2020" on TikTok and Instagram, and it instantly became a viral hit.

But the most significant viral media content of the year was also its saddest and most traumatizing: seventeen-year-old Darnella Frazier's video that captured the horrifying death of George Floyd on a Minneapolis street, as his breath expired under the weight of a police officer who pinned his neck to the ground. Her video added fuel to the #BlackLivesMatter movement.

People tried to understand the onslaught of events. The pandemic created renewed interest in movies like *Pandemic* (2016), *Contagion* (2011), and *Outbreak* (1995), as viewers confronted fictional accounts that suddenly seemed not so fictional.

On issues of racial justice, Americans looked for answers and put several books on the best-seller lists, including Ibram X. Kendi's *How to Be an Antiracist* (2019), Reni Eddo-Lodge's *Why I'm No Longer Talking to White People about Race* (2017), and Isabel Wilkerson's *Caste: The Origins of Our Discontents* (2020). People also turned to relevant movies, such as *Do the Right Thing* (1989), *Fruitvale Station* (2013), *13th* (2016), and *If Beale Street Could Talk* (2018).

Watchmen on HBO, which covered the almost-forgotten 1921 Tulsa massacre, in which white mobs destroyed a Black community and killed as many as three hundred people, led all television programs in the 2020 Emmy nominations and took home eleven awards. Similarly, the Pulitzer Prize–winning 1619 Project from Nikole Hannah-Jones of the *New York Times*, which marked the four-hundredth anniversary of the arrival of the first enslaved Africans to what would become the United States, continued to animate national discussions of Black history.

And, of course, many people spent the year experiencing the reality of wearing face masks, using lots of hand sanitizer, and engaging in the awkward communication of Zoom meetings. Digital media overwhelmed people in 2020, but it also provided ways to help them cope with the year's events and grapple with their history in the hope of better years to come.

 What media platforms did you use most often during the pandemic? Were these different media than you typically use? How did they help you cope with the events of 2020 and beyond?

Understanding the Media Today

In an age of economic and social upheaval, what should we expect from our media when it comes to capturing complex events and issues, from elections to pandemics to protests? At their best, media today in all their various forms—from mainstream news sites and radio talk shows to TikTok memes—can help us understand, or at least weather, the events that affect us. But at their worst, they can misrepresent or exploit tragedies in the process of documenting them. Many viewers and critics also disapprove of how the media, particularly TV and social media, hurtle from one event to another and, in so doing, often dwell on trivial celebrity-driven content.

In this book, we examine the history and business of mass media and discuss the media as a central force in shaping our culture and our democracy. This chapter starts by examining key concepts and introducing the critical process—a series of steps you can follow to think critically about the complex nature of the media. In later chapters, we probe the history and structure of our media's major institutions. In the process, we develop an informed and critical view of the influence these institutions have had on national and global life. The goal is to attain **media literacy**—to become critical consumers of media products and reflective users of media technologies by understanding how media construct meaning.

In this chapter, we will:

- Define key concepts, like communication, culture, mass media, mass communication, and masspersonal communication
- Investigate important periods in communication history: the oral, written, print, electronic, and digital eras
- Learn how the digital revolution and media convergence have shaped today's culture and media environment
- Learn about various tools that can help us think differently about media
- Consider key issues related to the politics of media representation and storytelling
- Discuss how the judgments we make about media reflect historically specific and political circumstances
- Study media literacy and the five stages of the critical process: description, analysis, interpretation, evaluation, and engagement

How We Got Here: Culture, Technology, and the Evolution of Media Communication

One way to understand the impact of media on our lives is to explore their relationship to culture. For some, the idea of culture brings to mind art, classical music, and fine literature—the often highly revered forms of creative expression that set standards about what is true and beautiful. Culture, however, can also be viewed more broadly as the ways in which people live and represent themselves in a particular society at a particular time. This idea of culture encompasses art, music, and literature, but also sports, fashion, architecture, education, religion, science, and, importantly for our purposes, the **mass media**—the industries that produce and distribute songs, video games, movies, novels, news, Internet services, and other cultural products to a large number of people.

Culture includes a society's beliefs, customs, rituals, games, technologies, traditions, and institutions. It also encompasses a society's modes of **communication**: the creation and use of symbol systems that convey information and meaning. While languages like English, Arabic, and American Sign Language are obvious symbol systems, the concept can be applied to any system we use to communicate, such as traffic lights, clothing, public restroom signs, or photographs.

Culture is made up of the products that a society creates. But culture is more than products

EXAMINING CULTURE *Parasite* (2019), a dark comedy about class differences from South Korean director Bong Joon-ho, won the Academy Award for best picture in 2020, illustrating the global nature of the film industry and the complexity of how media products and their values circulate today. What might this image say about the cultural values the film explores?

© Neon/Everett Collection, Inc.

alone; it also includes the processes that forge those products and the diverse values embedded in them. Thus, **culture** may be defined as the forms and systems of expression that individuals, groups, and societies use to make sense of daily life, communicate with other people, and articulate their values. According to this definition, when we upload selfies, listen to music, read books, watch television, play video games, or share memes, we are not usually asking "Is this art?" but are trying to identify or connect with something or someone through meaningful experiences.

Culture, therefore, is a process that delivers the values of a society through products and other meaning-making forms. It is also a political process through which competing values struggle, with some values becoming mainstream and others marginal. A society's ideas about what is important, normal, and moral are established, reinforced, and challenged through its culture. In this way, the media products we use and consume link us to our society by providing shared and contested values. For example, we might ponder how the American ideal of "rugged individualism," in which a heroic character overcomes villains or corruption, is reinforced or challenged through films like *Captain Marvel*, television shows like *Better Call Saul*, first-person shooter video games like *Call of Duty*, and various other media products.

Media technologies are another important part of a culture because they influence how people communicate with one another and how a society gathers, uses, transmits, and saves information. Different technologies have different **affordances**, which are the features or capabilities of a technology that help establish how we use it. What kind of information does a technology allow us to send, how quickly, in what form, and to whom? Does the technology make it possible to store information or not? Does it allow for one-way or two-way communication? Understanding the evolution of media technologies over the years helps us grasp more fully how our lives—and our society—are influenced by the technologies we use today. The historical development of media and communication can be traced through five overlapping eras in which emerging technologies disrupted and modified older forms of communication:

- The first two eras, oral and written, are most closely associated with the earliest human communities, where people communicated largely within tribal and feudal societies.
- The next two eras, print and electronic, fueled the growth of **mass communication**: the process of designing cultural messages and stories and delivering them to increasingly large and diverse audiences through mass media channels like newspapers, magazines, movies, radio, and television.
- Finally, the digital era—our current era—has unfolded alongside the rise of computer technologies and the Internet and has been marked by an ever more complex media environment. The distinction people once drew between *mass communication* (assumed to be one-to-many, public, impersonal, and produced by media industries) and *interpersonal communication* (assumed to be one-to-one, private, personal, and produced outside media industries) makes less sense now that digital tools like social media apps have altered how we communicate. New concepts like **masspersonal communication** are used to point out ways in which we communicate that mix and match aspects of mass and interpersonal communication.[2] For example, posting a birthday wish on someone's Facebook wall, where it can be seen by all their "friends," can be both deeply personal and relatively public—at least more so than sending a card by mail would be. Videos of wedding-proposal flash mobs posted to YouTube turn personal moments into public events.

MASSPERSONAL This widely circulated meme uses the hybrid nature of masspersonal communication for comic effect, pointing out that in the age of social media, our intimate Instagram posts function as someone else's favorite CW soap opera.

As we'll see in the sections that follow, the transitions that occur as we move from one era to the next are complex, taking decades or even centuries to play out. Older forms of communication don't disappear—we still talk to each other and handwrite notes—but a new era begins when the role played by one form of communication in a society is taken over by a new form. The rise of a new era of communication often coincides with a shift in how social power is distributed; those who control the means of communication can gain enormous political influence.

Oral and Written Eras in Communication

In most early societies, information first circulated through oral traditions. This reliance on verbal stories represents the first era of communication: the oral era. Without the ability to record information in written form, the primary way a community stores its knowledge is in people's memories—a situation that gives elders, poets, teachers, and storytellers an important cultural role.

Alphabets and the technologies of writing emerged in some cultures starting around 3000 BCE, but it took centuries or longer for a manuscript—or written—culture to overshadow oral customs. In ancient Greece, that shift didn't take place until after 1000 BCE, and in some societies, it never has. When the transition occurred in Greece, tensions between oral and written communication emerged. Philosophers who believed in the superiority of the oral tradition feared that the written word would weaken people's memories and undermine rigorous public discussion. Similar tensions or "moral panics" arise every time new communication technologies unsettle established norms and authorities. More recently, for example, some critics have argued that Twitter and online comment sections erode the quality of public debate.

In the written era, producing documents was expensive, requiring costly materials like ink and parchment as well as human labor; a document only existed if someone—a monk, a court scribe, or a philosopher—transcribed it by hand. These costs allowed rich and powerful institutions like the Catholic Church to gain centralized control over the production and circulation of manuscripts. In turn, this control over information distribution reinforced their political power. Working people, in contrast, were generally illiterate, and the economic and educational gap between rulers and the ruled was vast.

Christopher R. Martin

EARLY BOOKS Before the invention of the printing press, books were copied by hand in a labor-intensive process. This beautifully illuminated page is from a medieval Latin manuscript held at the Musée Marmottan Monet in Paris, France.

The Print Era

While forms of printing using wood-carved blocks developed in China around 1045, what we recognize as modern printing did not emerge until the middle of the fifteenth century, when Johannes Gutenberg, a German goldsmith, invented a printing press that used movable metal type. His invention ushered in the print era. Printing presses and print publications spread rapidly across Europe by the early sixteenth century. Eventually, books became one of the first mass-marketed products due to the combined benefits of the printing press:

- Machine duplication replaced the tedious system in which scribes hand-copied texts.
- Duplication could occur rapidly, so large quantities of the same book could be reproduced easily.
- The faster production of multiple copies brought down the cost of each unit, making books more affordable to less-affluent people.

These developments prompted several important changes throughout Europe, each of which ultimately affected the larger societal structure and cultural values.

Resistance to Authority

Since mass-produced printed materials could spread information and ideas faster and more widely than ever before, writers could use print to disseminate views counter to traditional civic and religious authority—views that paved the way for major social changes, such as the Protestant Reformation (which challenged the power of the Catholic Church in Europe), the growth of a middle-class business community, and the rise of modern nationalism, as people began to think of themselves as part of a country whose interests were distinct from local or regional concerns.

The Spread of Literacy

As much as they tried, it was difficult for religious, political, and business leaders to gain exclusive control over printing technology, at least in democratic societies. Instead, the mass publication of affordable pamphlets, magazines, and books in the United States helped democratize knowledge and increase literacy rates among the working and middle classes. The availability of printed literature and textbooks, combined with an emerging industrial economy in need of a more educated workforce, encouraged compulsory education, thus promoting literacy and extending learning beyond the world of wealthy upper-class citizens.

Focus on Individualism

The printing press also fostered the modern ideal of individualism. With access to wider sources of information that they could discover and read on their own, people came to rely less on their local community and religious, political, and business leaders for information and guidance, a shift that disrupted "the medieval sense of community."[3] By the mid-nineteenth century, the ideal of individualism increased resistance to government interference in the affairs of self-reliant entrepreneurs. The democratic impulse of individualism became a fundamental value in American society in the nineteenth and twentieth centuries.

The Electronic Era

The Industrial Revolution had an enormous impact on life in Europe and the United States. During the 1880s, for example, roughly 70 percent of Americans lived on farms and in small towns; by the 1920s, more than 50 percent were living in urban areas, where new industries and economic opportunities beckoned. Factories were replacing farms as centers of work and production, and the city began to overtake the country as the focal point of national life. This shift set the stage for the next era in mass communication—the electronic era—which saw the rise of new media technologies, corporate control of media, and widely shared media experiences.

Electronic Media Technologies

The gradual transformation from a print-based society to the electronic-based Information Age began with the development of the telegraph in the 1840s. The first technology to manipulate electricity as a means of communication over long distances, the telegraph worked by sending electrical signals over a network of wires. The telegraph made four key contributions to communication:

- Unencumbered by stagecoaches, ships, or the pony express, the telegraph separated messages from transportation, making communication almost instantaneous.[4]
- In combination with the rise of mass-marketed newspapers, it transformed "information into a commodity, a 'thing' that could be bought or sold irrespective of its uses or meaning."[5] By the time of the Civil War, news had become a valuable product.
- It made it easier for military, business, and political leaders to coordinate commercial and military operations on a national and—after the installation of the transatlantic cable in the 1860s—a global scale.
- It led to future electronic-based technologies, such as radio broadcasting (originally called *wireless telegraphy*), the fax machine, and the cell phone.

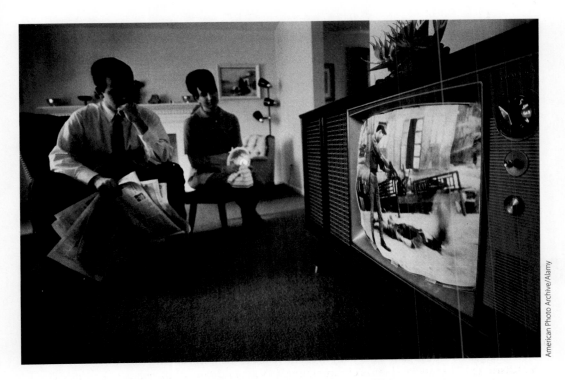

Other technologies also flourished during this time. Following a similar timeline to the telegraph, the development of various photography and audio recording technologies during the 1800s led to various image- and audio-rich innovations in the twentieth century. Visual and audio reproductions— including film and radio—transformed how people understood themselves, others, and their relationship to the world around them. They also changed how journalists covered wars, marketers sold products, and people remembered the past. The visual, aural, and electronic converged with the arrival of television in the 1950s, which became the era's dominant medium.

The Rise of Corporate Control

In the electronic era, communication systems were largely controlled by corporations. Unlike the relatively low cost of owning a printing press, building and maintaining national telecommunications and broadcasting networks required enormous financial resources. In the United States, large corporations like the American Telephone & Telegraph Company (AT&T) and the Radio Corporation of America (RCA) owned the infrastructure, a fact that centralized control of that technology and aspects of American culture in the hands of a few organizations and established a pattern that continues today with powerful digital-era corporations like Google, Facebook, and Amazon.

The Mass Nation

When used in conjunction with mass marketing strategies, electronic-era media like radio, film, and television helped establish what might be called a **mass nation**—a society in which a large percentage of a diverse population went to the same movies, listened to the same Top 40 hits, watched the same TV shows, and trusted the same evening news anchors. In the 1970s, when most households received only a handful of television channels, over 90 percent of Americans watching television on any given evening were tuned to one of three channels: ABC, NBC, or CBS.[6] For much of the twentieth century, the impact of the mass media helped establish powerful **consensus narratives**—stories that reflected certain values and assumptions about what the world is and should be like. In the process, they helped establish a mainstream American culture and identity. By the beginning of the twenty-first century, however, the Information Age had passed into its digital phase, changing society's relationship to media and culture once again.

The Digital Revolution

The digital revolution refers to a new way of converting, or *encoding*, information like images, text, or sounds into a format that can be saved and transmitted. **Digital communication** converts media content into combinations of ones and zeros (binary code) that are then reassembled, or *decoded*, when you play a video game on your console, view a picture on Instagram, or download a textbook to your laptop.

While the roots of digital communication can be traced back to the invention of the transistor in the 1940s (a key device in converting information to binary code), the transition to the digital era picked up speed in the 1980s, as home computer ownership grew, and in the 1990s, when the Internet became accessible to more and more people. Other milestones in the digital transition include the launch of Apple's iPhone in 2007 and the completion of the transition to all-digital television broadcasting in 2009. The next section explores the many dramatic changes brought about by this transition to the digital era.

Media in Our Digital Era

As happened with the development of the printing press in the 1400s and electronic communication technologies in the 1800s, the emergence of digital communication fundamentally disrupted existing media business models and cultural practices. It altered the ways we engage with media products and even changed how we organize our daily lives and relate to the world around us.

Convergence

Humans have always encoded (converted) information in order to transmit or save it. Spoken language is a form of encoding, for example, in that we convert the thoughts in our head into words we can express aloud. The evolution of communication technologies is partly the invention of new forms of encoding and decoding. In early photography, light was converted into images on a metal plate or paper using various chemicals. For decades, the sound waves of music were encoded by cutting grooves into vinyl discs and then decoded by a record player's needle.

Before the digital era, information was encoded in different and incompatible delivery formats: People watched television on a TV set, listened to music on a record player, watched movies at a theater, received letters through the mail, looked at pictures in a photo album, and so on. Today, because

MEDIA CONVERGENCE
In the past, media technologies like radios, film projectors, record players, telephones, and television sets were incompatible with one other, and media designed for each device would be consumed separately. Today, because of the digital transition, we can use a laptop or smartphone to listen to a radio talk show, watch a movie, stream a favorite song, call a friend, or binge-watch a series. And we can usually do those things from almost anywhere.

Everett Collection, Inc.

Jolemi Productions